Level 1 is
some initi
told very s
frequently repeated words.

Special features:

Opening pages introduce key story words

Careful match between story and pictures

Large, clear type

Educational Consultant:
Geraldine Taylor

A catalogue record for this book is available from the British Library

Published by Ladybird Books Ltd
80 Strand, London, WC2R 0RL
A Penguin Company

001 - 10 9 8 7 6 5 4 3 2 1

ISBN: 978-1-40930-711-2

Printed in China

The Emperor's New Clothes

Illustrated by Marina Le Ray

woman
man
boy

wife
clothes
Emperor

One day a man came to see the Emperor.

"I can make you some beautiful new clothes," said the man.

The next day the man came back.

"Do you like your beautiful new clothes?" he said. "Only clever people can see them."

"Yes," said the Emperor.

But he could not see any new clothes.

The Emperor saw his wife.

"Do you like my beautiful new clothes?" said the Emperor. "Only clever people can see them."

“Yes,” said his wife.

But she could not see the Emperor’s new clothes.

The Emperor saw a man.

"Do you like my beautiful new clothes?" said the Emperor. "Only clever people can see them."

"Yes," said the man.

But he could not see the Emperor's new clothes.

The Emperor saw a woman.

"Do you like my beautiful new clothes?" said the Emperor. "Only clever people can see them."

"Yes," said the woman.

But she could not see the Emperor's new clothes.

The Emperor saw a little boy.

"Do you like my beautiful new clothes?" said the Emperor. "Only clever people can see them."

"No," said the little boy. "You are not wearing any clothes."

"Oh no!" said the Emperor, and he ran all the way home.

How much do you remember about the story of The Emperor's New Clothes? Answer these questions and find out!

- Who came to see the Emperor?
- What was special about the beautiful new clothes?
- What did the little boy say to the Emperor?